W9-AAV-662

A Caribbean Journey from A to Y

(read and discover what happened to the Z)

Written by **Mario Picayo**

Illustrated by **Earleen Griswold**

campanita
BOOKS
NEW YORK

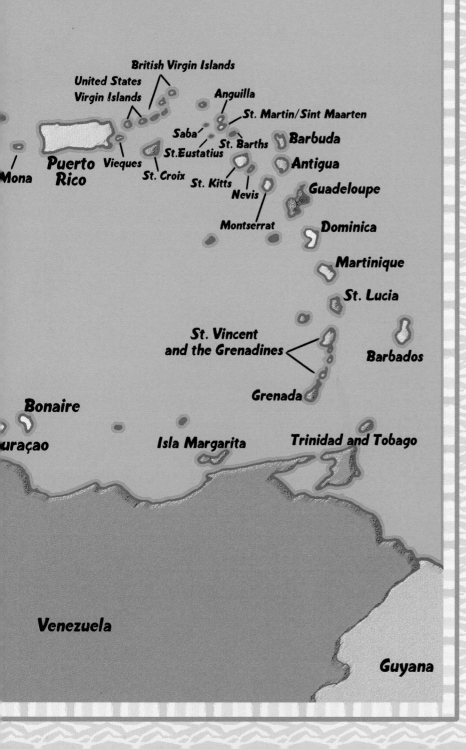

North

Atlantic Ocean

British Virgin Islands
United States
Virgin Islands
Anguilla
St. Martin/Sint Maarten
Saba
St. Barths
Barbuda
St.Eustatius
Antigua
Puerto Rico
Vieques
St. Croix
St. Kitts
Guadeloupe
Nevis
Mona
Montserrat
Dominica
Martinique
St. Lucia
St. Vincent and the Grenadines
Barbados
Grenada
Bonaire
Curaçao
Isla Margarita
Trinidad and Tobago
Venezuela
Guyana

Find these places on the map:

Anguilla
Antigua and Barbuda
Aruba
Bahamas
Barbados
Belize
Bermuda
Bonaire
British Virgin Islands
Cayman Islands
Colombia
Costa Rica
Cozumel
Cuba
Curaçao
Dominica
Dominican Republic
Florida (USA)
Gonâve
Grenada
Guadeloupe
Guatemala
Guyana
Haiti
Honduras
Isla de la Juventud
Isla Margarita
Jamaica
Martinique
Mexico
Mona
Montserrat
Panama
Puerto Rico
Saba
St. Barthelemy/St. Barths
St. Croix
St. Eustatius/Statia
St. Kitts and Nevis
St. Lucia
St. Martin/Sint Maarten
St. Vincent and the Grenadines
Trinidad and Tobago
Turks and Caicos
United States Virgin Islands
Venezuela
Vieques

Library of Congress Cataloging-in-Publication Data

Picayo, Mario, 1957-
  A Caribbean journey from A to Y : read and discover what
happened to the Z / Mario Picayo ; illustrated by Earleen
Griswold. -- 1st ed.
    p. cm.
  ISBN-13: 978-0-9725611-8-1 (hardcover : alk. paper)
  ISBN-10: 0-9725611-8-8 (hardcover : alk. paper)
  1. Caribbean Area--Miscellanea--Juvenile literature. I.
Griswold, Earleen, 1965- II. Title.
  F2161.5.P5313 2007
  972.9--dc22

Dedication

From the Author:
To my children,
to Carla, and to the
Caribbean and its people,
my inspiration and my
roots.

From the Illustrator:
To Ashley, Kara, and Don,
the loves of my life. To the
very special people that
made my illustrations
possible and my years
in the Virgin Islands
unforgettable.

Dear Reader,

There are over seven thousand islands, islets, reefs, and cayes in the Caribbean Sea, and its waters touch several countries in North, Central, and South America. You will soon realize, as we travel from **A** to **Y**, that our trip is limited to some of those islands. I included the names of many of them, but I could not name them all. My apologies to all the ones I missed.

I also stretched the definition of "Caribbean" a bit and included islands that are not in the Caribbean Sea. Nevertheless, they share enough history and cultural traits with the "real" Caribbean that they are considered sister islands. The Bahamas and the Turks and Caicos are next-door neighbors, and Bermuda, even though it's farther north in the Atlantic, needs to be included for the same reasons. "Caribbean" is not just a geographical space, it's also a space of mind and heart.

Enjoy!
Mario

If you want to learn much more about the Caribbean and about the words included in this alphabet journey, visit www.editorialcampana.com.

 **is the first letter of the alphabet.**

Aruba, Anguilla, Antigua, and Anegada all begin with the letter A.
So does Antilles, as our Caribbean islands are called.
A is the letter for airplane, which we all love to ride and watch flying in the sky.
It is for the delicious avocado, and also for animals like ants and alligators.

Abaco
Andros

B is for boat. Our islands were originally inhabited by people who came in boats of many sizes.

It is for bananas. Do you know anyone who doesn't like bananas?

It is the letter for beach, our favorite playground.

And for boy.

It is also the letter for beans.

Did you know that there are black beans, red beans, white beans, pink beans, green beans, pinto beans, lima beans, and even jumping beans?

Do you know of any other kind of bean?

Barbados
Bequia
Bermuda
Bimini
Bonaire

 reminds us of good things to eat, like cookies and coconuts.

It reminds us of fun times of the year, like Carnival and Christmas.
C is the letter for a frog that lives in Puerto Rico, the coquí (or coki), and for two huge reptiles, the crocodile and the caiman. It is for crab, the little crustacean with the big claws, and also for car. There are toy cars and real cars — which ones do you like best? It is the letter for our good friend, the rainmaking cloud, and of course, it is the letter for Caribbean.

Carricou
Cayo Romano
Cayman
Cuba
Culebra
Curaçao

**D** is for Dominica, the island with 365 rivers (or close to that), where the Carib Indians live.

It is for some mammals, like dog, deer, and donkey.
Delicate dragonfly begins with D.
It is also the letter for drums: bongo drums, conga drums, steel drums — we love drums!
And for divers, diving under our clear waters to enjoy the wonders of the sea.

Dominica

Dominican Republic

 **is for egret, a white bird that you will see near cows many times during the day, or by the water at dawn and dusk.**

It is for egg, from which all birds and many other creatures hatch.

It is also for equator. Do you know where the equator is? Just a hint: it is not too far from the Caribbean.

Eleuthera

 **is for frog and for friend.**

We can have fun with our friends.
We can go fishing or climb big **Flamboyant
Trees.**
F is the letter for father, and also for flags.
The ones shown here represent
many Caribbean islands.
It is also the letter for freedom.

G is for girl. Are you a girl?

It is for fragrant gardenia and for delicious guava.
It is the letter for goat, a very useful animal that lives on many of our islands.
Instruments like the guitar and the güiro begin with **G**.

Gonâve
Grenada
Guadeloupe
Great Exuma

H is for home and also for house.

Do you know the difference between the two?

It is for harbor. Boats and ships enter harbors in order to reach our shores and to seek protection from the force of the mighty hurricane.

H is the letter for some birds, like the powerful hawk, and for the smallest of them all, the hummingbird.

It is for the helpful horse and for one of our favorite flowers, the hibiscus.

And for hammock. It is so nice to fall asleep in a hammock.

Haiti

I is for islands, where many of us live, and for indigenous people, the islands' first inhabitants.

(Amerindian is another name for the Caribbean's indigenous people.)

I is the letter for insect. Bees, mosquitoes, and butterflies are insects. So are cockroaches, but not spiders. How come?

It is for pretty birds like the ibis, and for prehistoric-looking reptiles like the iguana.

Isla de la Juventud

Isla Margarita

is the letter for joy and for justice.

For sweet-smelling jasmine and for refreshing juice.
And remember, if you go in the ocean, watch out for stinging jellyfish!

Jamaica
Jost Van Dyke

K is for kites, how beautiful they look dancing in the wind!

It is the letter for key, which can open and close the doors to houses and cars. What else can you open and close with keys?
K is also the letter for two beautiful birds, the kingfisher and the kestrel.

 is for friendly little lizards.

And for lobster. Have you ever seen a lobster?
It is also the letter for love, our favorite emotion.

Long Island

 **M** is for mongoose.

And for delicious mango.
It is the letter for mountain. Many of our islands have mountains. Some of them we can climb (if they are not too steep).
And let's not forget two very important Ms: mother and music.

Marie Galante

Martinique

Mayaguana

Mona Island

Montserrat

Mustique

 **N** is the letter for nutmeg.

Nutmeg is a very important fruit (and seed) for many countries, like Grenada, and it is sold around the world.
It is also the letter for nest, where most birds are born.

Nevis

O is for orchid, one of the prettiest flowers in the world.

O is for birds like owls and oystercatchers. It is also the letter for ocean, and for two of its inhabitants, the oyster and the eight-legged octopus.

P is for pelican, the bird with the long beak and the pouch that we see by the beach diving for fish.

And for parrot. We have parrots in many Caribbean islands. Isn't it amazing how they can talk and sing?
It is the letter for three delicious fruits: papaya, pineapple, and passion fruit.
It is also the letter for peace.

Puerto Rico

 is for quiet, like our nights.

is for rain, which we all need to live.

And what follows many rains? Beautiful rainbows!

It is for rocket ship, which astronauts use to ride into space, like we see in the movies. There is an astronaut from the Caribbean; do you know from which island? (Hint: it starts with a C and it's very big.)

R is the letter for exercises like running and rowing, and also the letter for resting — what we do after a long day (and after a short day too!).

S

S has to be one of our favorite letters.

It is the letter for sand, sea, sun, and sailboat.
For star and sky.
For sweet sugarcane.
For sound and for song.
For mighty shark and friendly seal.
We used to have seals in the Caribbean,
but not anymore (maybe there are
a few around).
It is also the letter for the name of many
of our islands. (By the way, "St." stands for
"Saint," so St. Lucia is really "Saint Lucia.")
S is also the letter for one of the saddest of
words: slavery.

Saba

San Salvador

Sandy Cay

St. Barths

St. Croix

St. Eustatius

St. John

St. Kitts

St. Lucia

St. Martin

St. Thomas

St. Vincent and
the Grenadines

 **T** is for toucan, a very pretty bird that we can find in Trinidad and Tobago.

It is for turtle and tortoise. Do you know the difference between them?
It is for tamarind, which we eat and from which we make juice.
It is for the tropics, where the Caribbean is.
It is also the letter for tree, trunk, and thorn — ouch!

Tortola
Turks and Caicos

 **U** is for urchin, like the sea urchin, which clings to the rocks by the seashore.

It is for umbrella, good under the hot sun or the pouring rain.

Union Island

 **is for volcano.**

Many of our islands are extinct volcanoes, but
many volcanoes are still active.
It is for visitors, as we call the people
who come from all over the world
to meet us and see our islands.
It is for voice, which we use to speak and sing.

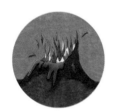

Vieques
Virgin Gorda

 **is the letter for water, which we drink when thirsty, and where we swim, play, and sail.**

It is for whale, like the humpback, which visits us every year.
It is also a good letter for asking questions, like **Who, What, Where, When,** and **Why?**

 **X** is the letter for xylophone, an instrument that many of us can play.

When we write xxx at the end of a letter to a friend, it means kisses. Isn't that funny?

 **is for yes, a word we all like to say and hear.**

It is for edible roots like the yam and the yucca.

Z is the last letter in our alphabet.

What words begin with Z?
Zoo begins with Z, but we'd rather use it for zebra.
We don't have zebras in the Caribbean (except at the zoo), but that doesn't matter.
We will take our Z to Africa, where zebras are really from, and where they still run free.
Zulu, Zaire, Zambia, and Zimbabwe also start with the letter Z. And so does the name of beautiful Zanzibar.

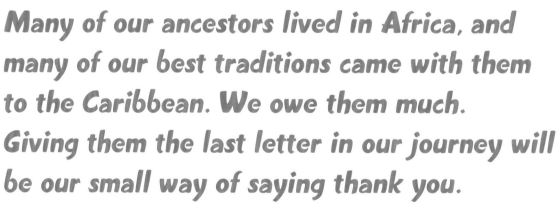

Many of our ancestors lived in Africa, and many of our best traditions came with them to the Caribbean. We owe them much.
Giving them the last letter in our journey will be our small way of saying thank you.

Afterword from the author

I was born and raised in the Spanish-speaking Caribbean (Cuba and Puerto Rico), made my home as an adult on an English-speaking island (St. Thomas, U.S. Virgin Islands), and I've had the good fortune of getting to know the Greater Antilles, and many of the Lesser Antilles, intimately. As you travel in this beautiful part of the planet, and as you get to know each island nation, you come to understand at an intellectual, emotional, and spiritual level that what separates us most is not the water. Language and politics obscure our cultural and historical similarities, and create an illusory sense of distance. We know more about faraway lands — England, France, and the United States in particular — than we know about our own neighbors, whether we speak about the islands around us or the countries that share the Caribbean Sea with us, like Belize, Colombia, Costa Rica, Honduras, Mexico, Nicaragua, and Venezuela, to name some.

I wanted to write a children's book that represented our reality from the perspective of a native, and I also wanted to include a few facts about our part of the world that would surprise and amuse.

Some islands have alligators, others grow nutmeg, and most celebrate Carnival. Many of us know about sea urchins, mangoes, and hammocks. But I am sure that most will be surprised to discover that Dominica claims to have as many rivers as there are days in the year, or that the Caribbean has its own astronaut (Cuba's Arnaldo Tamayo-Méndez is not just our only astronaut, but is also the first person of African descent to fly into space).

This book celebrates everything that makes each island unique and special, but also recognizes our many similarities. I hope that at some level, regardless of how small, I have succeeded in what perhaps was my ultimate intention, to bring our islands and our people a little closer.

Mario Picayo,

January 2007

About the Author

MARIO PICAYO was born in Cuba, grew up in Puerto Rico, and lived a large part of his adult life in the U.S. Virgin Islands. He is a cultural activist, audiovisual artist, and producer. When not in New York, Mario can be found somewhere in the world (most likely the Caribbean) with his cameras and notebook at a cultural celebration, such as Carnival. He has worked for the Smithsonian Institution, the Dominican Republic's Institute of Folklore, and many other cultural organizations in the United States and the Caribbean. Mario also worked for Sesame Workshop (Sesame Street) as Spanish Editor in their magazine division. In 2004, the New York State Assembly made public recognition of his artistic career and of his work as a defender and promoter of Latino and Caribbean culture. In 2006 he became a grandfather.
You can write to Mario at: mario@editorialcampana.com

About the Illustrator

Native American artist **EARLEEN GRISWOLD** is a west coast resident who lived for five years in St. Thomas, U.S. Virgin Islands, where she met Mario, and where the illustrations for this book were born. She lives in Washington state with her husband Don and their two daughters Ashley and Kara. This is her first published work. Earleen and Don are the owners and managers of the Old Liberty Theater in Ridgefield, Washington. Take a virtual tour at: www.oldlibertytheater.com.
Write to Earleen at: earleen@editorialcampana.com

About the Book Designer

YOLANDA V. FUNDORA is a Cuban-American artist who currently lives in Chatham, New Jersey. She designed the book and cover using patterns belonging to her textile collections. Yolanda's fine-art work is part of many private and corporate collections. She has been Featured Artist for Apple Computer's iCard series, has had a long career as an illustrator and product designer in the gift and toy industry, and currently runs her own licensing studio. To see her fine-art work, visit her website: www.yolandafundora.com. To see her textile lines, visit: www.loveinstitches.com.

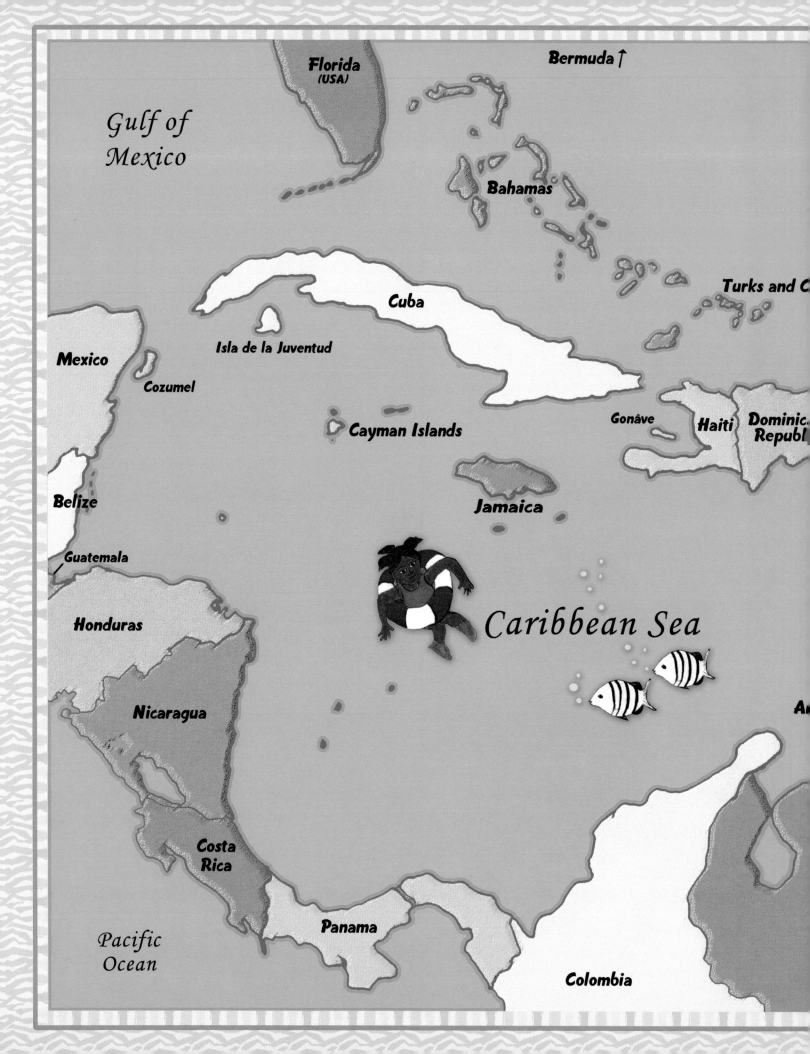

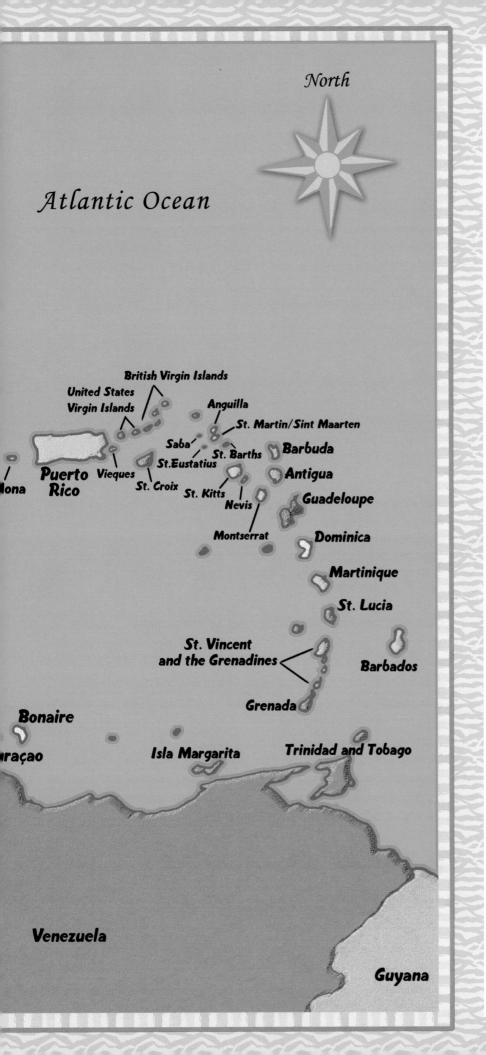

North

Atlantic Ocean

British Virgin Islands
United States
Virgin Islands
Anguilla
St. Martin/Sint Maarten
Saba
St. Barths
Barbuda
St.Eustatius
Antigua
Puerto   Vieques
Rico
St. Croix
St. Kitts
Nevis
Guadeloupe
Mona
Montserrat
Dominica
Martinique
St. Lucia
St. Vincent
and the Grenadines
Barbados
Grenada
Bonaire
Isla Margarita
Trinidad and Tobago
uraçao
Venezuela
Guyana

Find these places on the map:

Anguilla
Antigua and Barbuda
Aruba
Bahamas
Barbados
Belize
Bermuda
Bonaire
British Virgin Islands
Cayman Islands
Colombia
Costa Rica
Cozumel
Cuba
Curaçao
Dominica
Dominican Republic
Florida (USA)
Gonâve
Grenada
Guadeloupe
Guatemala
Guyana
Haiti
Honduras
Isla de la Juventud
Isla Margarita
Jamaica
Martinique
Mexico
Mona
Montserrat
Panama
Puerto Rico
Saba
St. Barthelemy/St. Barths
St. Croix
St. Eustatius/Statia
St. Kitts and Nevis
St. Lucia
St. Martin/Sint Maarten
St. Vincent and the Grenadines
Trinidad and Tobago
Turks and Caicos
United States Virgin Islands
Venezuela
Vieques

Other titles by Campanita Books

My Brain Won't Float Away / *Mi cerebro no va a salir flotando*
Written by Annette Pérez
Illustrated by Yolanda V. Fundora
Translated by Jacqueline Herranz-Brooks
Language: Bilingual: English and Spanish
ISBN: 978-0-9725611-2-9 (0-9725611-2-9)

Annie, an eight-year-old girl, gathers the courage to ask her mother, "Why is one of my hands smaller than the other? Why do I fall so much?" What follows is a story of fears, will, self discovery, and finally, triumph. Annette Pérez narrates her true story of growing up with hydrocephalus with humor, honesty, and compassion, and proves with this story that even the simplest act can change one's life forever.

Annie, una niña de ocho años, finalmente se atreve a preguntar a su mamá: ¿Por qué tengo una mano más pequeña que la otra? ¿Por qué me caigo tantas veces? Lo que sigue es una historia de descubrimiento de ella misma, de temor, fuerza de voluntad y finalmente, de triunfo. Annette Pérez, quien padece de hidrocefalia, cuenta su niñez con humor, honestidad y compasión, y prueba con su historia que a veces un acto muy sencillo puede cambiar tu vida para siempre.

A Very Smart Cat / *Una gata muy inteligente*
Written by Saldemar Kent
Illustrated by Yolanda V. Fundora
Translated by Jacqueline Herranz-Brooks
Language: Bilingual: English and Spanish
ISBN: 978-1-934370-00-1 (1-934370-00-2)

Meet the smartest cat in the world. She can draw, knows how to make phone calls, can take pictures, and plays musical instruments. Do you want her? She is yours. Free! Read the funny and surprising adventures of this extraordinary pussycat and you will understand why sometimes there is such a thing as being too smart. A very, very funny book about a very, very clever cat.

Te presentamos a la gata más inteligente del mundo. Sabe dibujar, llamar por teléfono, sacar fotos, y tocar instrumentos musicales. ¿La quieres? Es tuya. ¡Gratis! Lee las chistosas, y sorprendentes, aventuras de esta extraordinaria gatita y comprenderás por qué a veces se puede ser "más listo de la cuenta". Este es un libro muy, muy chistoso acerca de una gata muy, muy lista.

Campanita Books are available at: www.editorialcampana.com and from your favorite bookseller.